WEATHER

By

Steffi Cavell-Clarke

©2017
Book Life
King's Lynn
Norfolk PE30 4LS

ISBN: 978-1-78637-214-7

Written by:
Steffi Cavell-Clarke

Edited by:
Charlie Ogden

Designed by:
Evie Wright

A catalogue record for this book
is available from the British Library

PHOTO CREDITS

CONTENTS

Words that look like this can be found in the glossary on page 24.

What Is SCIENCE?

What should I wear when it's raining?

What is weather?

How many types of weather are there?

Science can help us to answer many difficult questions. It can also help us to understand the world around us.

What Is WEATHER?

Weather is all around us. There are many different types of weather. For example, the weather can be sunny or cloudy.

The weather is not the same everywhere. It can be cloudy in one area of a country, but sunny in another part of the same country.

7

SUNSHINE

Never look directly at the Sun.

When there are few clouds in the sky and the Sun is out, we say that the weather is sunny. The sunshine feels warm on your skin.

When it is sunny, people often spend time outdoors.
Most people wear light clothing to keep themselves cool.

It is often sunny in the summertime.

9

CLOUDS

When there are lots of clouds in the sky, we say that it is cloudy. A cloud is a large group of water droplets in the sky.

There are different types of cloud. Clouds that float high in the sky are often thin. Clouds that are low in the sky are often fluffy.

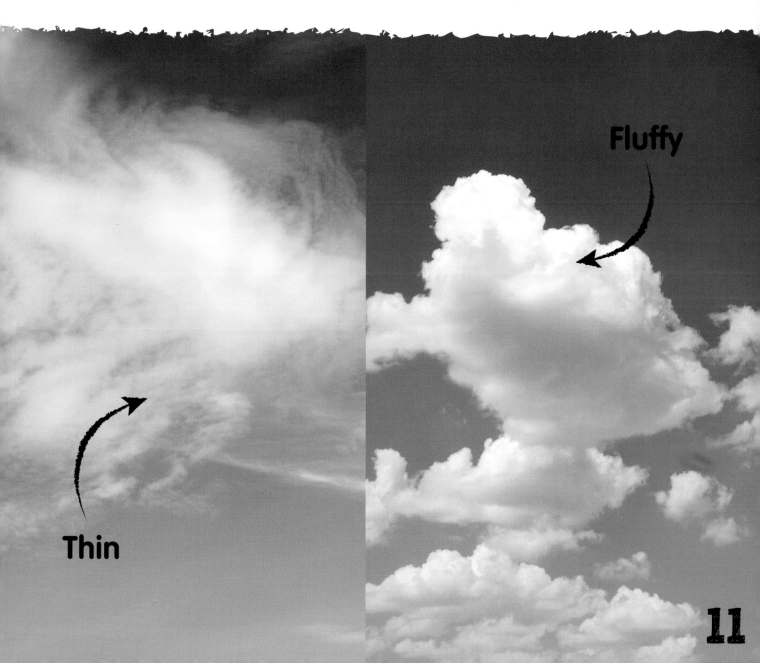

Fluffy

Thin

RAIN

When it rains, lots of tiny water drops fall from the clouds. Sometimes clouds make a lot of rain and sometimes they make none at all.

Many people wear wellington boots and carry an umbrella when they go outside in the rain.

Umbrellas are **waterproof**.

SNOW

It mostly snows during winter.

When it gets very cold, rain can **freeze**. We call the frozen rain snow.

It is important to wear warm clothes when it snows. Many people wear hats and gloves.

WIND

The wind is air that moves around the planet.
You can't see the wind, but you can feel it.

Wind can sometimes be very strong. Sometimes, the wind is so strong that it blows down whole trees.

A strong wind is called a gale.

17

THUNDER AND LIGHTNING

Lightning

Lightning is a bright flash of **electricity** that usually happens during a **thunderstorm**.

Lightning makes a sound called thunder. Thunder can sound like a sharp crack or a low rumble.

19

EXTREME WEATHER

The weather can sometimes be very dangerous. Very heavy rains can cause flooding. Flooding can destroy homes and farms.

20

If it doesn't rain for a very long time, it can cause a **drought**. When there is a drought, rivers can dry up and leave many places without water.

Let's
EXPERIMENT!

You need a responsible adult to help you!

STEP 1

Get an adult to pour five centimetres of hot water into the glass jar.

STEP 2

Cover the jar with the plate and wait a few minutes.

22

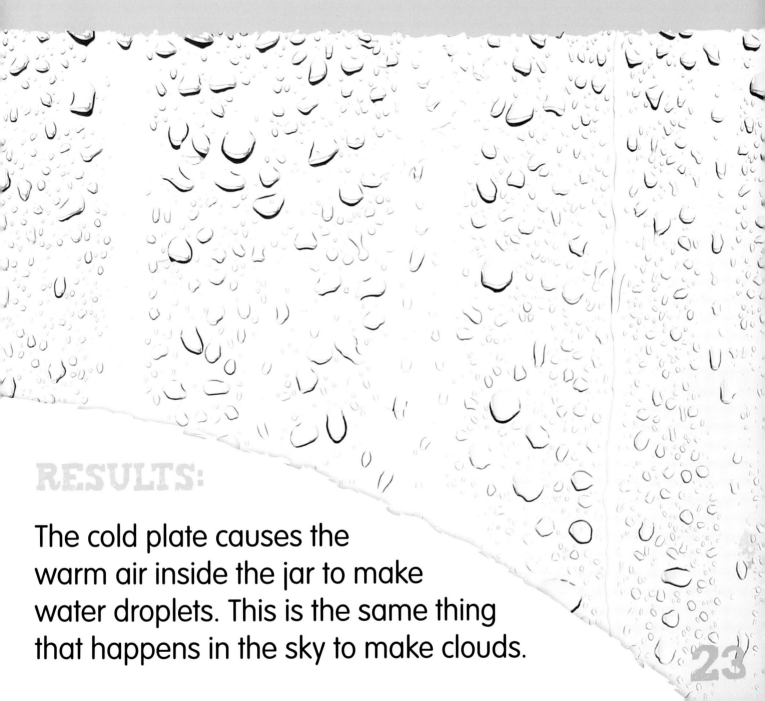

RESULTS:

The cold plate causes the
warm air inside the jar to make
water droplets. This is the same thing
that happens in the sky to make clouds.

GLOSSARY

droplets	very small drops of liquid
drought	a long period with very little rainfall
electricity	a type of energy
flooding	dangerous, overflowing water
freeze	turn to ice
thunderstorm	a storm with thunder and lightning
waterproof	resistant to water

INDEX